T0398784

My Short U Words

Consultants

Ashley Bishop, Ed.D.
Sue Bishop, M.E.D.

Publishing Credits

Dona Herweck Rice, *Editor-in-Chief*

Robin Erickson, *Production Director*

Lee Aucoin, *Creative Director*

Sharon Coan, *Project Manager*

Jamey Acosta, *Editor*

Rachelle Cracchiolo, M.A.Ed., *Publisher*

Teacher Created Materials

5301 Oceanus Drive
Huntington Beach, CA 92649-1030
http://www.tcmpub.com
ISBN 978-1-4333-2566-3

I like the **umbrella**.

I like the tr**u**nk.

I like the b**u**tter.

I like the tub.

I like the bus.

I like the cup.

I like the truck.

I like the duck.

I like the nuts.

Glossary

b**u**s   b**u**tter   c**u**p

d**u**ck   n**u**ts   tr**u**ck

tr**u**nk   t**u**b   **u**mbrella

Sight Words

I   like   the

Activities

- Read the book aloud to your child, pointing to the short *u* words as you say them. After reading each page, ask, "What do you like?"

- Have your child help you paint a plain coffee mug to decorate it. Remind him or her that the word *mug* has the short *u* sound.

- If your child has never been on a bus, go with him or her somewhere on the bus. Let him or her help you give the bus fare to the bus driver.

- Have your child think of other short *u* words and draw pictures of them to make his or her own word book. Suggest examples if the child cannot think of any.

- Help your child think of a personally valuable word to represent the short *u* sound, such as *uncle*.